Never Lost

Heather Turpin Ziegman

BookLeaf Publishing

India | USA | UK

Made with ❤ on the BookLeaf Publishing Platform
www.bookleafpub.in
www.bookleafpub.com

Dedication

Josef, Eli, and Scarlett
...because having you means
I am never lost.

Preface

Acknowledgements

1. Rainy Days

I long for rainy days.
Natures gift of peace.
When everything is in it's place,
and emotions are in line.
Allowing me to do the very thing
I'm being called to do,
be still.
Feeling frantic on those days
is like going against nature.
There is a silent message
of calm in the air,
telling me to rest my mind.

2. Ticking Clocks and Faucets Dripping

The house is quiet,
and the sky is gray.
Rain is slowly falling.
The lights are off,
and the curtains pulled back.
Outside gloom fills only open
areas of the house.
Deepened nooks in rooms not used
remain still.
Only vast shadows.
A small space of comfort
where everyone sits.
Meanwhile, echos of ticking clocks
and faucets dripping
in rooms with no light
remain comfortably in place.
There's a certain peace from the calm
in the still shadows of these rooms
that on another day,
will be filled with light.
We sit for now,
in our small space,

in our dim house,
in the rain.

3. Lost/Home

You may feel lost at times,
that to continue on doesn't seem worth it.
But to them,
you are their home.
You are what makes them feel worth it,
so they don't feel lost.

4. The Smell of Home

It's the simple things,
most wouldn't give a second thought.
Like the smell of home on his skin,
his clothes,
and in his hair.
Only then to realize,
it no longer smells like the home
he once shared with you.

5. Haunting Intuition

Wonderful noise to a haunting silence
stuns my heart with pain and guilt.
An intuition embedded in the bond
between mother and child.
The ache kills me
but you, my dear,
is what keeps me going.
I will forever bare the broken
so you can remain whole.

6. Emotions Left Stagnent

I had failed to see the magnitude
of these unprocessed emotions left stagnent
and how they crept through
every tiny seam.
Eventually, it would consume
every inch of me.
I would be left to face it alone,
in a world unfamiliar.
Hope ran thin of ever seeing light again,
but I got back up.

7. The Last Betrayal

Because I'll never know
if your true intentions
are covered
by sympathetic words.

8. Mend Whats Broken

Show me your heart
and convince me its mine.
Take what you want
then leave me stranded
without a second thought.
I'll bend morals
and sacrifice myself.
You'll use me again and again.
I see you, but,
you only see yourself.
Your intentions aren't to fix what you've broken.
Instead you leave the shattered pieces for another day.
But as you walk away this time,
don't expect to come back to shattered glass.
Because I'm good at fixing what others have left for
nothing.
So after I mend what's broken,
Your unreliable hands will never hold me again.

9. Letting Go

I couldn't see past the guilt.
I was falling, rapidly.
No matter what I did,
it was never enough.
Until I was finally able to let go.
Loosening my grip on the manipulative
hand that promised me comfort
but kept me in darkness
for all these years.
I've learned that the fight alone
was enough
to never give up.

10. Fear of Water

I dreamed of a time
which was once reality
just out of reach.
A place I can no longer return to,
the boy who no longer exists.
Stolen somewhere through time,
slipped away while I wasn't looking.
"Where did it all go?"
I ask this new, unfamiliar face.
"...and where are you going to now?"
"Somewhere new." you say,
"But I still need you.
Take my hand and we'll dive in together."

11. Blue Hour Drive

The sky is a deep hush,
a lingering shade of night
holding on before the sun arrives.

The road is empty,
washed in the softest blue,
where headlights feel too harsh,
cutting through the quiet.

Buildings emerge from shadow,
edges sharpening with the slow crawl of light.
Streetlights flicker out,
one by one,
like stars surrendering to dawn.

The air is cool,
heavy with the scent of stillness,
of something just beginning.

I keep driving,
watching the world wake up,
feeling the weight of a moment
that will vanish too soon.

12. The Weight of Silence

There are days when the silence is heavier than stone,
pressing into my ribs,
settling in the hollow places where words once lived.

I move through rooms filled with echoes,
shadows of voices that no longer call my name.
The air tastes of yesterday,
of things I meant to say but never did.

Grief does not knock.
It slips in through the cracks,
settles in the spaces between heartbeats,
becomes the rhythm of my breathing.

I tell myself that time is a river,
that it will carry me forward,
but some moments do not flow—
they linger,
root themselves in the marrow of my bones.

And so I sit in the quiet,
letting it unfold around me,
letting it remind me
that love, once given, never really leaves.

13. The Boy and the Troll

Deep in the woods where the tall trees grow,
A little boy wandered, quiet and slow.
The air smelled of pine, the earth damp and cool,
And just past the creek sat a moss-covered stool.

Upon it, hunched low, with eyes deep and old,
Was a troll made of stone, with a heart made of gold.
His hands rough as bark, his grin wide and bright,
Yet kindness still flickered like soft morning light.

The boy did not run, nor shrink back in fear,
He stepped even closer and whispered, "You're here."
The troll gave a chuckle, low and profound,
"I've sat in these woods where the lost can be found."

They talked about stars, about birds in the trees,
About rivers that whispered their tales to the breeze.
The boy told of worries too heavy to hold,
The troll listened gently, his warmth breaking cold.

And when it was time for the boy to go home,
He promised the troll he'd never be alone.
For deep in the woods, past the creek's silver roll,
A boy had befriended a kind-hearted troll.

14. She is the Storm

She came into this world like a wildfire,
eyes burning with a light too bright to tame.
Even as a child, she walked with the weight of ancient
stars,
small hands gripping the edge of the universe,
daring it to shift beneath her feet.

She does not ask for permission.
She does not wait to be told.
She carves her name into the wind,
leaves footprints in stone,
laughs in the face of thunder.

There is a wildness in her that cannot be silenced,
a beauty that does not beg to be understood.
She is the storm and the calm after it,
the fire and the ashes that bloom into something new.

I watch her move through the world,
unapologetic, fierce,
and I know—
nothing will break her that she will not rebuild.

15. Between Them and the Dark

She watches the world sharpen its teeth,
a shadow stretching toward her children,
cold hands reaching for what she swore
she would always keep safe.

She places herself in the way,
though she is no wall, no weapon,
only flesh, only trembling hands
that have held them since their first breath.

She pleads with forces that do not listen,
pushes back against tides that do not yield,
carries their fear on her back
until her spine bends,
until her body becomes the barricade
between them and the dark.

But love is not armor.
It cannot stop the unseen,
cannot silence the hunger of fate
or the cruel indifference of the world.

Still, she fights,

because surrender is a word
her heart does not understand.

17

16. Footsteps in the Fog

The path bends where the light fades,
soft earth sinking beneath small feet.
Trees lean in, their branches whispering,
but the boy walks on, unafraid.

Something waits beyond the mist,
not darkness, not fear—
but a presence, quiet and vast,
like the hush before rain.

A hand, rough like stone,
reaches through the veil of gray.
The boy takes it,
and the world feels lighter.

17. But Always, I Find You

I have known you before—
in the hush of ancient forests,
where our laughter tangled in the wind
like wild vines reaching for the sun.

I have found you again—
in cities of stone and flickering lanterns,
where our hands brushed in a crowded street,
and something in me remembered.

I have lost you, over and over,
watched time pull you away like a tide,
felt the echo of your name
in lifetimes where we never spoke.

But always, I find you.
In a glance that lingers too long,
in a voice that feels like home,
in a love that never truly left.

And if the stars burn out,
if the world begins again,
I know I will search for you,
and I know you will be waiting.

18. The Fire

It happened fast—
flames licking the walls,
smoke curling like a whisper of warning.
The air turned thick, heavy with loss,
and then, just like that,
everything was gone.

The photographs melted into memory,
pages of books curled like dying leaves.
Clothes, blankets, the old wooden chair
where laughter once sat—
all turned to ash.

I stand where the door used to be,
feet sinking into the blackened remains,
and wonder how emptiness
can feel so heavy.

But somewhere in the ruins,
the wind stirs the soot,
and I swear I hear a voice—
soft, steady,
telling me to begin again.

19. Loving You To Leave

The years slip by like sand in streams,
A blur of laughter, fading dreams.
Tiny hands once held so tight,
Now reach for stars in endless flight.

I watch you grow, I watch you change,
A little more, a little strange.
The boy I knew, now not the same,
Chasing dreams that I can't name.

Your steps grow sure, your heart more wide,
No longer needing me beside.
But still I grieve, a quiet ache,
For every moment you must take.

The crayons fade, the toys are gone,
And in their place, a world you're on.
I long for days of sleepy sighs,
When you would rest beneath my eyes.

Yet in my heart, I know it's right—
You must unfold, you must take flight.
Still, each goodbye, each turning page,
Tugs at the soul, ignites the stage.

So I'll hold you close, in memory's thread,
And let you grow, though tears are shed.
For you, my child, will always be
The one who lives inside of me.

20. Meet Me in the Forest

Gloom hangs in the air under the overcast sky.
You're both at recess at a new school
but you miss the familiarity of home.
You miss her.
You're confused about why everything changed
and how you ended up here.
More than any length of distance
or any amount of time
the bond you both share with her
is embedded deep in your soul
where it's been since you were first housed in her womb.
There is a knowing
and you glance at one another
assured you're both feeling the same thing.
Sharing a slight nod
you both know it's time.
Without saying a word
you slowly wander away from the crowd of children
careful not to be noticed.
As you make your way from the playground to the tree
line
you hear the distant sound of the school bell ring.
Recess is over and all the kids hurry inside.
You see a teacher quickly scan the empty playground

as you both enter the forest.
You begin to walk
and after what feels like forever
of traveling deeper and deeper
you find a small clearing
with a moss covered log.
You tell your brother,
"She'll find us here."
After waiting patiently
echoes of twigs snapping.
Movement.
It's her.
Longing for this moment alone
she kneels down in front of you.
Placing both of your hands in hers
she gently says,
"Let's go home"

21. The Door in the Trees

They found it by accident,
just past the old oak
where the roots curled like fingers
around the edge of the world.

Three sets of footsteps—
one careful, one quick, one small—
pressed into moss that glowed beneath them,
breathless with discovery.

The air shimmered like heat on pavement,
but cool as river stones,
and when they stepped through,
the forest sighed,
as if it had been waiting.

A sky too wide to be real
stretched above castles made of mist,
rivers that sang their names,
fields where the wind carried laughter
from something unseen.

They ran,
they reached,

they believed—
and so the world grew around them,
threaded with their wonder.

But when the first light of evening
pooled at their feet,
they felt the pull—
the hush of home calling them back.

With one last look,
they stepped through the trees,
mud on their shoes,
leaves in their hair,
and the quiet knowledge
that the door would always be there
if they wished hard enough.

www.ingramcontent.com/pod-product-compliance
Lightning Source LLC
LaVergne TN
LVHW021332200726

843509LV00014B/2503